The
SUPER SMART
SPACE
Activity
Book

By Lisa Regan

Illustrated by
Emma Trithart

ARCTURUS

ARCTURUS

This edition published in 2022 by Arcturus Publishing Limited
26/27 Bickels Yard, 151—153 Bermondsey Street,
London SE1 3HA

Author: Lisa Regan
Illustrator: Emma Trithart
Editor: Violet Peto
Science Consultant: Anne Rooney
Designer: Sarah Fountain
Design Manager: Jessica Holliland
Managing Editor: Joe Harris

ISBN: 978-1-3988-1534-6
CH010096NT
Supplier 29, Date 0322, PI 00000706

Printed in China

What is STEM?

STEM is a world-wide initiative
that aims to cultivate an
interest in Science, Technology,
Engineering, and Mathematics,
in an effort to promote these
disciplines to as wide a variety of
students as possible.

OUR AWESOME UNIVERSE

From missions and moons to satellites and stars, this activity book launches you into space on a fact-packed tour of the universe and beyond. There are over 50 fun puzzles to solve and many out-of-this-world facts to discover along the way!

Did you know?

More than 18,300 people applied to NASA in 2017 and only 12 of them graduated as astronauts.

Find out if you have what it takes to become an astronaut with spot-the-difference scenes, logic puzzles, mazes, and more!

What are you waiting for? Turn the page and shoot for the stars!

DIAMOND STORM

Certain parts of our Solar System have rain showers of diamonds! Can you find three identical pairs of diamonds hidden among all the others?

Lightning storms on Jupiter and Saturn turn methane gas into carbon (in the form of soot). When it falls, it turns into diamonds.

LIFE IN SPACE

Astronauts spend months at a time on board the ISS (International Space Station). Can you order the six astronauts named below based on how much time each of them has spent in space?

* Yuri, Mike, and Peggy have spent the most time in space.
* Koichi has been there for longer than Sandra.
* Sunita has spent longer in space than Koichi.
* Mike is the longest-serving of them all.
* Yuri has been on board for less time than Peggy.

Astronauts' workday is from around 6 in the morning to 9:30 at night, with around 2.5 hours for exercise during that time.

Yuri

Peggy

Sunita

Mike

Sandra

Koichi

WHERE AM I?

A network of satellites links together to help us navigate here on Earth. These satellites are orbiting our planet. Can you spot the odd one out?

These GPS (Global Positioning System) satellites were first used by the military but now provide a service to all kinds of people.

GPS satellites allow us to do fun activities such as geocaching and playing Pokémon Go.

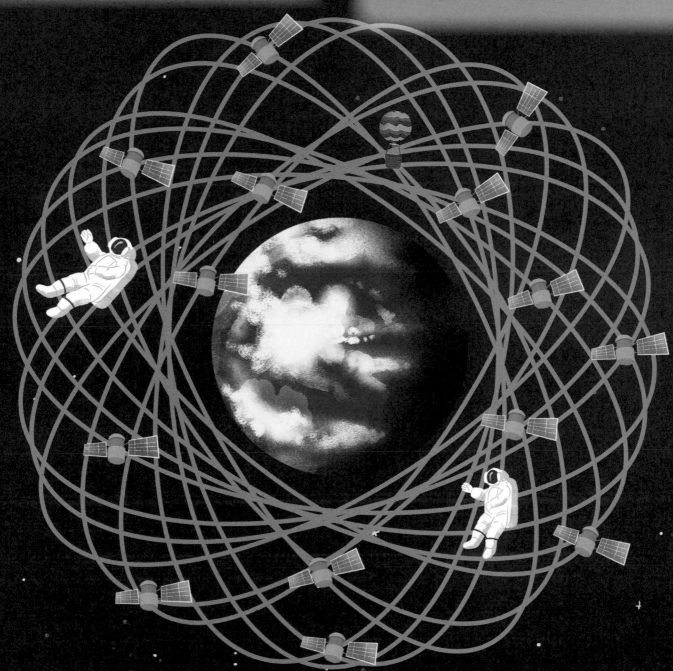

MISSION CONTROL

Astronauts working and living in space have an enormous team supporting them, here on Earth. Can you rearrange the panels to show the complete control room scene? Write the correct number order from left to right.

1   2   3   4   5   6   7   8   9   10

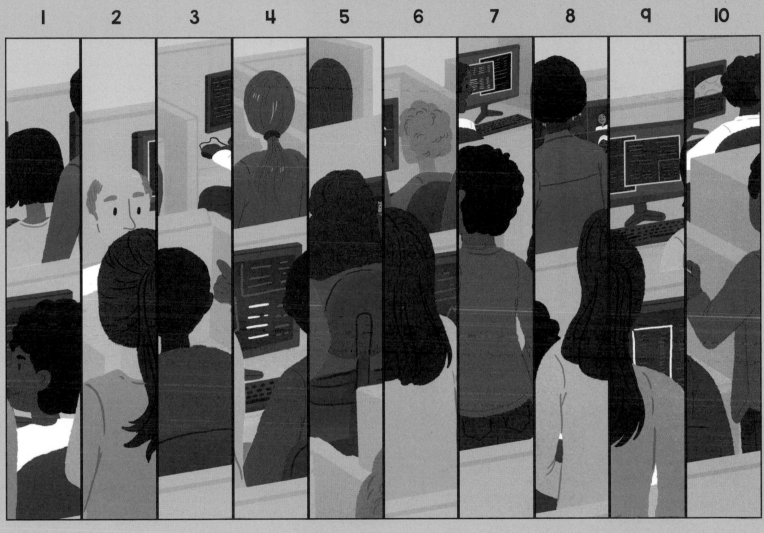

Many of the backup team for ISS and other NASA missions work in the Mission Control Room at the Johnson Space Center in Houston, Texas. They are responsible for planning the missions and checking that everything goes smoothly during the missions.

IN THE DOCK

A Russian spacecraft called Soyuz carries people and supplies to the space station. You can see it here, docked to the ISS. Look carefully at the two pictures and find ten differences between them.

8

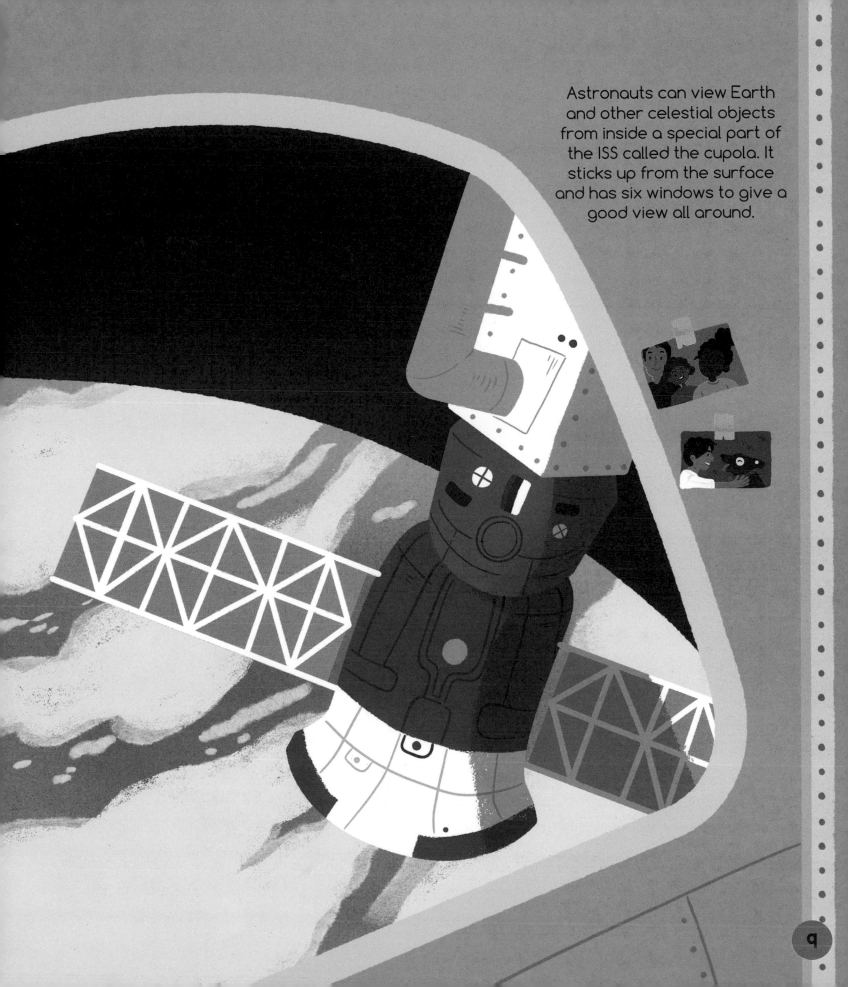

Astronauts can view Earth and other celestial objects from inside a special part of the ISS called the cupola. It sticks up from the surface and has six windows to give a good view all around.

SPIRALS IN THE SKY

Galaxies are grouped into four basic shapes, but the most familiar is the spiral. Match each of these galaxies into pairs and find one that isn't like any other.

The astronomer Edwin Hubble developed a system to categorize the shapes of galaxies. The shapes are spiral, barred spiral, elliptical, and irregular.

SMART SUIT

A space suit keeps an astronaut alive in space. Its made up of different specialist parts. Use pens or crayons to match the parts to the correct places in the space suit.

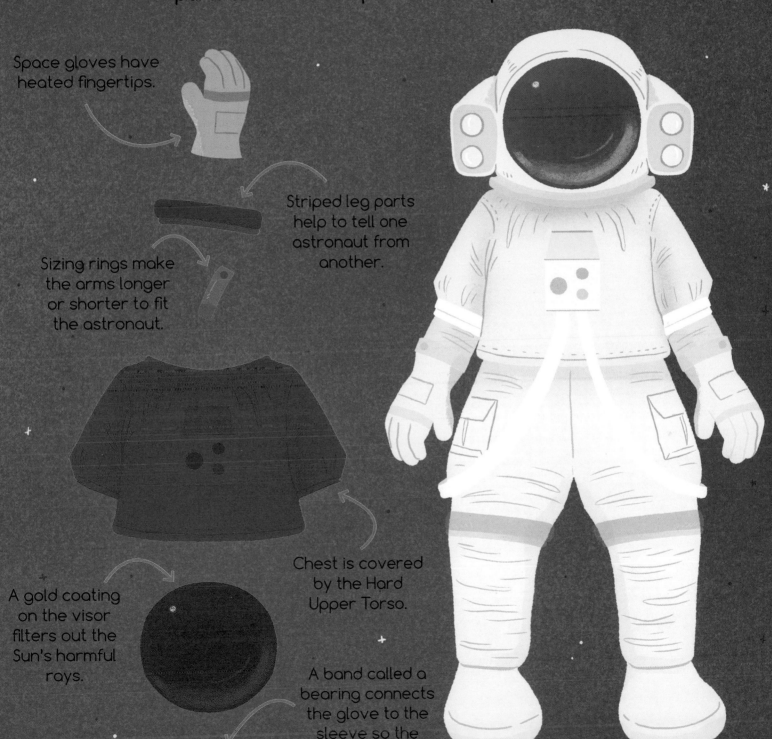

Space gloves have heated fingertips.

Striped leg parts help to tell one astronaut from another.

Sizing rings make the arms longer or shorter to fit the astronaut.

Chest is covered by the Hard Upper Torso.

A gold coating on the visor filters out the Sun's harmful rays.

A band called a bearing connects the glove to the sleeve so the wrist can turn.

LOST IN SPACE

These tools have floated away from the tool boxes on the space station. If each astronaut should have a full set of tools, how many items are missing?

It's one thing using ordinary tools inside the space station, but astronauts have special tools for use outside the craft. They have limited movement in their spacesuit, wearing thick gloves, so their tools are specially adapted.

Full set of tools

SPACE JUNK

Space may be huge—but it's far from empty. Can you help this astronaut find her way through the maze, collecting all the pieces of space junk? Be careful to avoid the asteroids!

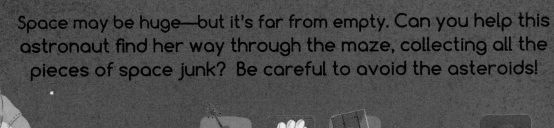

Space Junk

Asteroid

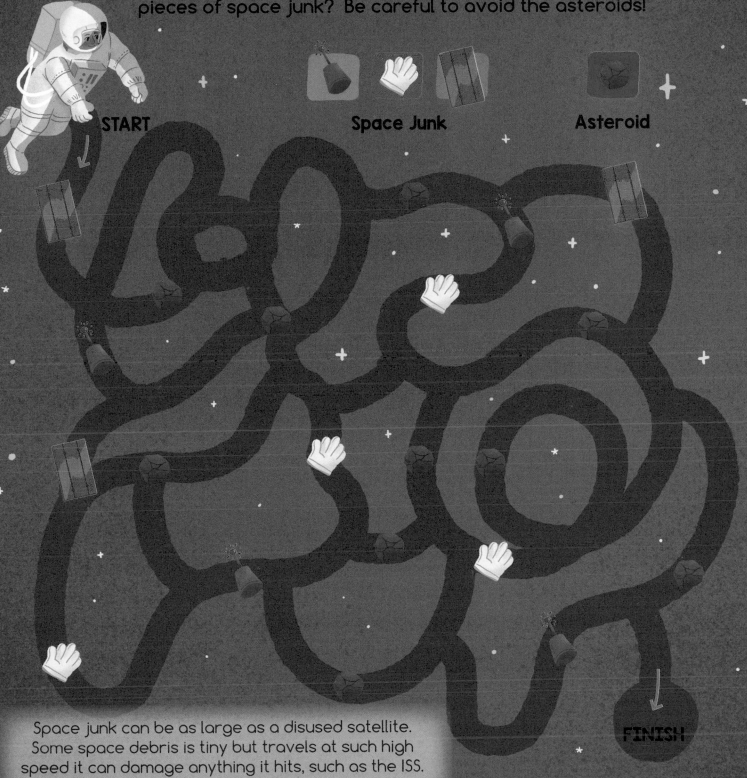

START

FINISH

Space junk can be as large as a disused satellite. Some space debris is tiny but travels at such high speed it can damage anything it hits, such as the ISS.

SPOT THE DIFFERENCE

Astronauts can live on board the International Space Station for weeks or even months at a time!

Can you spot eight differences between these two pictures from inside the space station?

APOLLO MISSIONS

People went to the Moon on a series of Apollo spacecraft. Use the key to locate and shade in some of the different sections of this Apollo command module.

Key:
- **1** = docking probe
- **2** = fuel cells
- **3** = liquid oxygen and hydrogen tanks
- **4** = high-gain antenna
- **5** = reaction control jets
- **6** = service module engine fuel tanks
- **7** = service module engine
- **8** = nozzle extension skirt

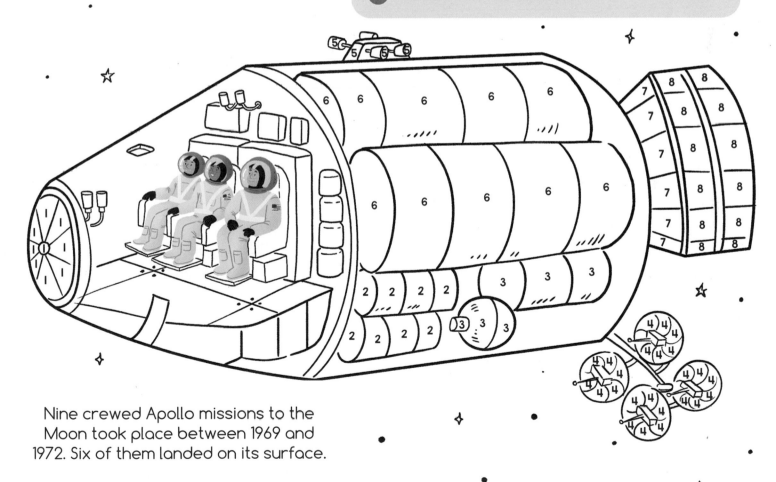

Nine crewed Apollo missions to the Moon took place between 1969 and 1972. Six of them landed on its surface.

A HELPING HAND

The Canadarm is an important piece of kit. It is a remote-controlled mechanical arm that can be used in space. Which of the boxes contains all of the parts to make the robotic arm?

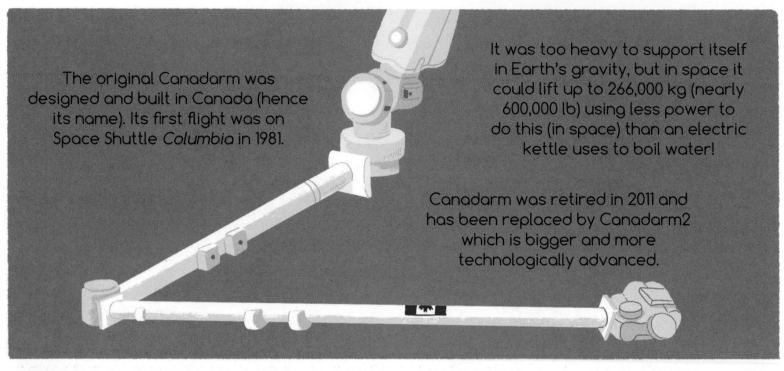

The original Canadarm was designed and built in Canada (hence its name). Its first flight was on Space Shuttle *Columbia* in 1981.

It was too heavy to support itself in Earth's gravity, but in space it could lift up to 266,000 kg (nearly 600,000 lb) using less power to do this (in space) than an electric kettle uses to boil water!

Canadarm was retired in 2011 and has been replaced by Canadarm2 which is bigger and more technologically advanced.

A
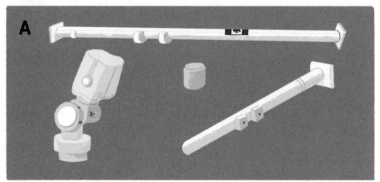

B
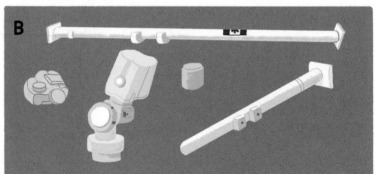

C
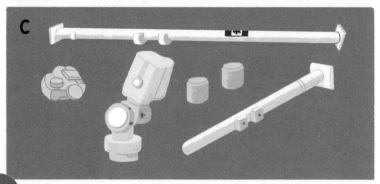

D
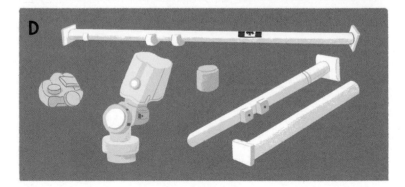

SMALL WORLDS

There are eight planets in our Solar System, but there are also some others that are a bit smaller and classified as dwarf planets. Find the names of two dwarf planets by crossing out any letter that appears more than once in each group. Use the remaining letters to spell the names.

TNMHAEHURIMSNAUT

WMAPKELWUMATOKE

There are five named dwarf planets but scientists think there may be more than a hundred more to be classified or discovered.

Pluto used to count as the ninth planet in the Solar System but was downgraded to a dwarf planet in 2006.

HUMANS ON THE MOON

The first people walked on the Moon in 1969. They were part of NASA's Apollo 11 mission. Which of the tiles below are not from the Apollo 11 crew photo on the next page?

The crew consisted of three astronauts: Buzz Aldrin, Neil Armstrong, and Michael Collins. Armstrong and Aldrin left the spacecraft to land on the Moon, while Collins stayed onboard to pilot the command module.

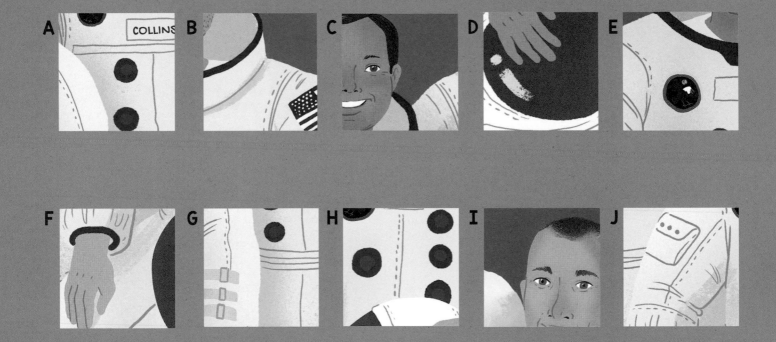

The Apollo 11 spacecraft was launched from Cape Kennedy in Florida on a Saturn V rocket on July 16, 1969.

Landing on the Moon was a big deal. The USA and the Soviet Union (now Russia) both wanted to be the first to achieve it and prove their technological superiority.

HUMAN COMPUTERS

How good at calculations are you? Work out what each symbol is worth so you can answer the final question below.

 $= 21$

$\star + \text{moon} + \text{moon} = 15$

$\text{planet} - \text{moon} = 8$

In the early days of space exploration, NASA employed a team of female mathematicians (including Katherine Johnson, shown here) to do their complex calculations. They were often worked out using pencil and paper.

After the introduction of actual computers, the teams of women helped program the computers and worked on the launches for the moon landings.

What is

$\text{planet} - \star + \text{moon} = $ ☐

HEY, ROVER!

A space rover is a vehicle designed to land on the surface of a moon, planet, or asteroid. They are amazing! See if you can spot seven differences between these two pictures.

Perseverance is a six-wheeled rover that landed on Mars in February 2021. It is being used to explore a crater on the surface of the red planet.

DISTANT STARS

Some of the biggest telescopes on Earth collect radio waves from stars, galaxies, and black holes in deep space. They are called radio telescopes.

Study the clues to figure out the correct order of these five telescopes from biggest to smallest.

* The Effelsberg Telescope in Germany is the second-largest.
* The Lovell Telescope in England is bigger than the DSS in Australia and the Sardinia Radio Telescope.
* The Australian telescope is smaller than the Sardinian one.
* FAST in China is bigger than the Effelsberg Telescope.

Radio telescopes often use huge dish antennae to collect radio waves. They can be over 30 m (100 ft) wide. Sometimes a group of dishes is used together to make a gigantic telescope.

REWIRED!

Many astronauts have a degree in engineering and electronics. Help this person do a little rewiring onboard!

* Which of the wires connects A to F?
* Which of the wires is loose and needs reconnecting?
* How many wires from B are connected to an orange terminal?
* Which battery needs changing to make the green light work?
* How many striped wires are there?

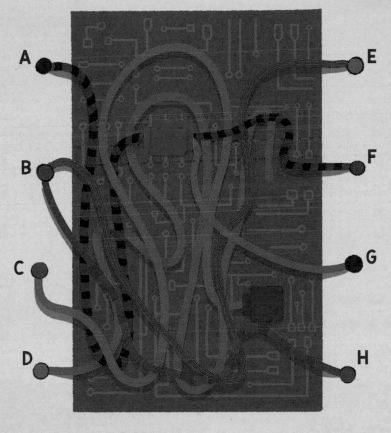

Astronauts train for months so that they can carry out any repairs needed. Sometimes these are onboard, but at other times, the astronaut has to leave the craft and spacewalk to fix the problem.

ONE GIANT LEAP

The first person to walk on the Moon was Neil Armstrong. He and fellow astronaut Buzz Aldrin carried out some simple scientific tests and collected rock samples. Follow the footprints to find the path from the flag back to the lunar module.

When Aldrin and Armstrong landed on the Moon in 1969, they spent 21 hours on its surface. They even slept there in the lunar module for seven hours!

Neil Armstrong made the first footprint on the rock dust of Moon's surface. As there is no wind to blow it away, it will be there for thousands or even millions of years.

START

When Armstrong landed, he famously said, "That's one small step for a man, one giant leap for mankind."

FINISH

Among other things, the astronauts left an American flag and also a patch to remember astronauts that were killed in an earlier Apollo mission.

A MATTER OF MASS

Objects weigh different amounts on different planets—but they always have the same mass. Work out the mass of each of the shapes.

Mass is the amount of material an object contains. It doesn't change even if you are on the Moon, on Jupiter, or orbiting the Earth.

COMET CLOUD

The Oort cloud is the most distant part of our Solar System. It is filled with billions of pieces of space debris and comets. Can you spot a comet that has changed direction to escape from the Oort cloud?

A comet is like a space snowball made of ice (frozen gas), dust, and rock. They can be a few miles wide or as big as a small town.

When a comet heats up, it forms a tail of gas and dust.

LIFE ON THE ISS

Study the clues and find the items in the picture that the astronauts need to stay clean and healthy in space.

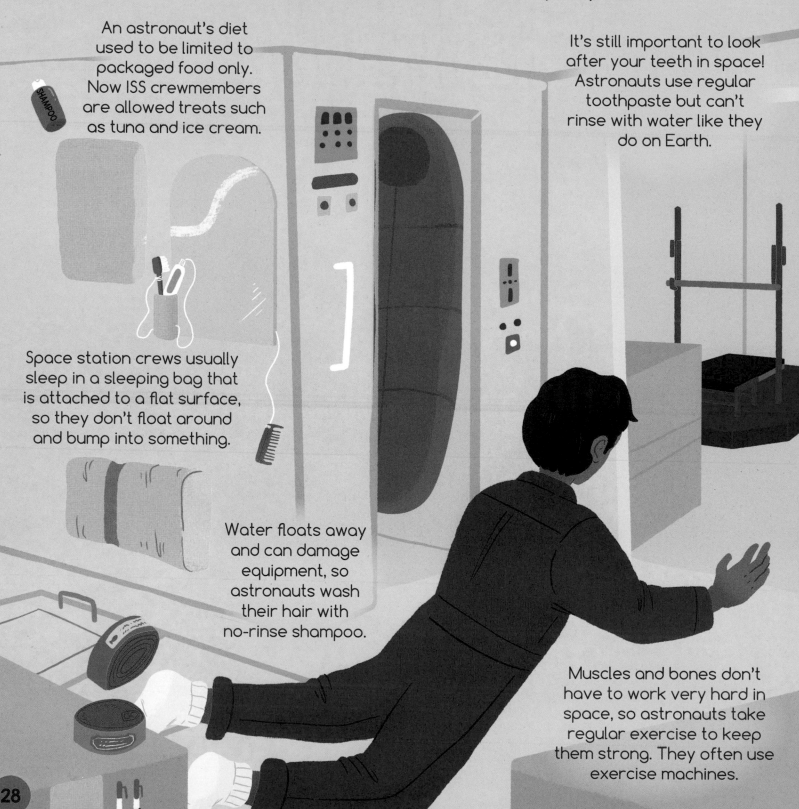

An astronaut's diet used to be limited to packaged food only. Now ISS crewmembers are allowed treats such as tuna and ice cream.

It's still important to look after your teeth in space! Astronauts use regular toothpaste but can't rinse with water like they do on Earth.

Space station crews usually sleep in a sleeping bag that is attached to a flat surface, so they don't float around and bump into something.

Water floats away and can damage equipment, so astronauts wash their hair with no-rinse shampoo.

Muscles and bones don't have to work very hard in space, so astronauts take regular exercise to keep them strong. They often use exercise machines.

SHAMPOO

CHOOSE ME!

Thousands of people want to be part of NASA's astronaut class—but very few can realize their dream. Narrow down the numbers by following the instructions.

* Half of these applicants don't have the right qualifications. Cross them out if they have a star on their suit.

* Now cross out any with a blue suit.

* Put a cross on one third of the remaining candidates.

* Circle a fifth of the remaining people. These are the successful candidates—how many are there?

Out of more than 12,000 applicants, NASA chose just 10 new astronauts for its 2021 candidate class.

SPACE FIX

Sometimes repairs need to be made to complex equipment. An astronaut may even do a spacewalk for external repairs. Help to figure this one out. If wheel A is turned clockwise, which way will wheel B move?

The white suits worn outside the ISS are called EMUs (extravehicular mobility units). On Earth, they are very heavy, but in space they weigh almost nothing.

An EMU has lots of different layers to keep an astronaut safe. These include heating and cooling layers and a special suit that allows the astronaut to pee while they're busy outside the ISS!

SPACE PARTS

How much is each part of this space rover worth?
Read equations A, B, and C, then solve equation D.

A.

wheel + wheel + wheel = 24

B.

umbrella + umbrella − wheel = 12

A lunar roving vehicle (LRV) is specially designed to drive around on the surface of the Moon. Three different LRVs have been sent to the Moon on separate missions.

C.

umbrella + camera = 17

D.

The LRV folds up to be stored in a small space for transportation to the Moon.

wheel + camera + umbrella = ☐

The vehicle was designed to make it much quicker and easier for astronauts to do research on the Moon.

FOOD FOR THOUGHT

NASA is interested in finding how plants grow in space.
Help the astronaut find the plants on the list.

The ISS has a "space garden" onboard, which houses the APH (Advanced Plant Habitat). The aim is to grow edible plants using LED lights instead of sunlight.

Chives

Lettuce

Peas

Oregano

Tomatoes

DOGS IN SPACE!

In 1961, Yuri Gagarin became the first human in space—but 48 dogs had already been in space before him! Use the clues to fill in the grid and work out when these five launched on their expeditions.

LAIKA

* Belka and Strelka went into space together.
* Laika was not the first dog in space.
* Dezik and Tsygan launched together, in the 1950s.
* Laika went up before Belka and Strelka.

	Belka	Strelka	Laika	Dezik	Tsygan
1951					
1957					
1960					

The longest canine spaceflight was a 21-day orbit by Veterok and Ubolyok.

The dogs were used as test subjects to see whether living beings could survive a trip into space.

Tsygan and Desik's space trip lasted 15 minutes and they landed safely back to Earth in their space cabin, slowed by a parachute.

COMING AND GOING

Astronauts travel to and from the ISS in a Russian spacecraft called Soyuz. Follow the Soyuz rockets through the grid to get from Earth to the ISS. Each move must follow a rocket from tail to tip.

ISS

A Soyuz spacecraft is made of two sections—the capsule and the rocket. The capsule has enough room to carry three people.

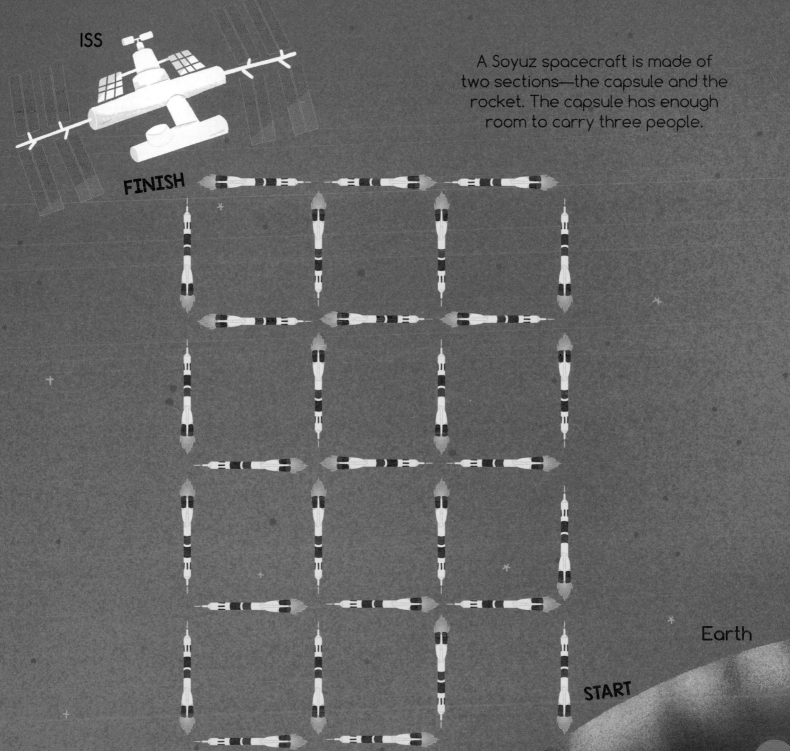

FINISH

Earth

START

SEEING STARS

Galaxies are made up of lots and lots of stars. Scientists estimate there are 100—400 billion stars just in the Milky Way galaxy. Can you find three of each of these stars?

Star chart

A star is a large ball of gas that gives off heat and light.

Stars come in different sizes. Our Sun is a medium-sized star.

36

SUPER STARS

Our Sun is a type of star known as a main sequence star but there are other types of star, too. Look at these star types and then turn the page.

A white dwarf star is no longer converting hydrogen into helium. It will eventually cool and fade.

A main sequence star like the Sun shines bright because it is converting hydrogen into helium and releasing huge amounts of energy.

Which stars have been added? How many have disappeared?

Red dwarf stars are the most common type of star. They are much cooler than our Sun.

Supergiants are the largest stars in the Universe. They consume hydrogen much faster than main sequence stars and so don't last for as long.

Some stars are bigger than the Sun. When they run out of fuel, they explode and become very dense neutron stars and the biggest become black holes.

GAS GIANT

Jupiter is the biggest planet in our Solar System. It is an amazing place. Which is the only group of letters that can be rearranged to spell JUPITER correctly?

TRIPEJU

UPJPITE

JRITERU

A year on Jupiter is the same as 11.8 Earth years but a day is just 10 hours long.

JEROPIT

Jupiter is the fifth planet from the Sun, and is made mostly of the gases hydrogen and helium.

UERJPPIT

PITEJUER

Jupiter has many moons orbiting it. Scientists keep finding and naming new ones but so far it has 79 confirmed moons.

AGAIN AND AGAIN

NASA's Space Shuttle looked like a plane but could be sent into space.
It landed like a plane, too, so it could be reused, unlike spacecraft before it.
Look carefully to find one of these shuttles that is a little bit different.

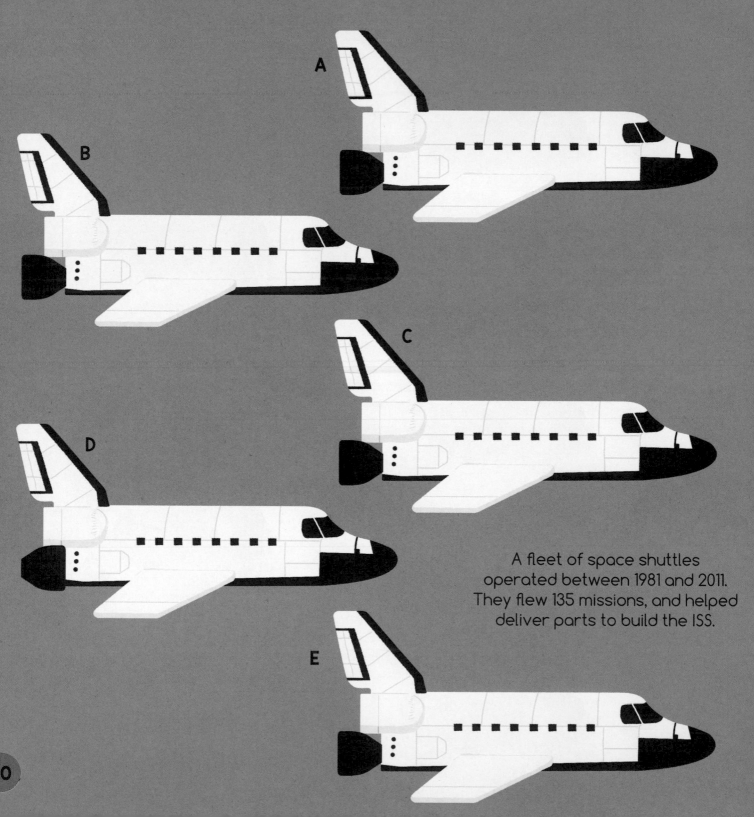

A fleet of space shuttles
operated between 1981 and 2011.
They flew 135 missions, and helped
deliver parts to build the ISS.

MERCURY MISSION

BepiColombo is a mission launched in 2018 to orbit and study the planet Mercury. Which of the kits below contains all the correct parts to build the mission's orbiters?

Mercury is the smallest planet, and the closest to the Sun.

BepiColombo involves two combined orbiters that will study the planet's surface and its atmosphere.

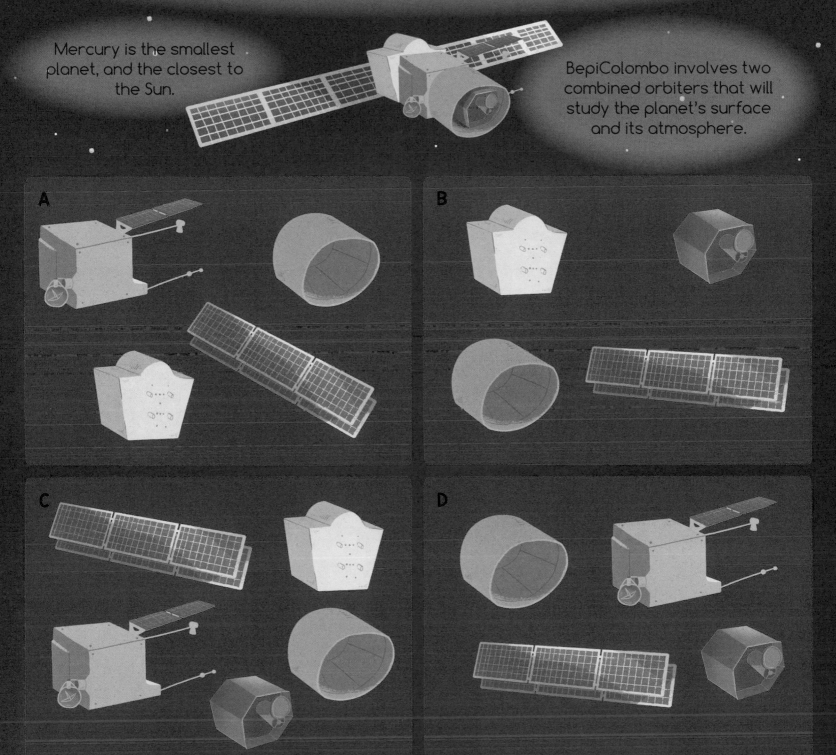

JOURNEY INTO SPACE

Imagine taking a train ride into space ... it might one day be possible! Space elevators will carry passengers far out into space more cheaply and easily than a rocket launch. Look at these two artists' impressions and try to find eight differences.

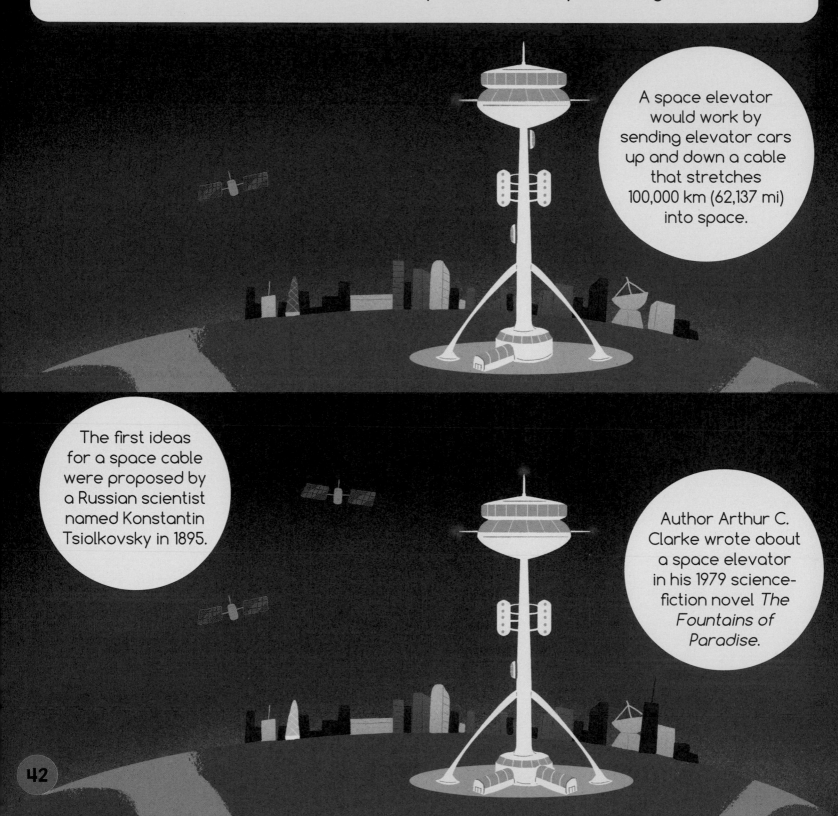

A space elevator would work by sending elevator cars up and down a cable that stretches 100,000 km (62,137 mi) into space.

The first ideas for a space cable were proposed by a Russian scientist named Konstantin Tsiolkovsky in 1895.

Author Arthur C. Clarke wrote about a space elevator in his 1979 science-fiction novel *The Fountains of Paradise.*

ORION MISSIONS

NASA is building a new spacecraft that will carry people deep into space. It is called Orion and is still in development. Which silhouette exactly matches the spacecraft?

Orion missions will launch from NASA's Kennedy Space Center spaceport in Florida.

Orion is designed with three main parts: a crew module, a service module, and a launch abort system (LAS). This LAS section comes away after Orion reaches orbit.

The crew module has space for up to four astronauts.

A

B

C

D

TWINS!

The constellation of Gemini is one of the zodiac family of constellations that was recorded in the second century by Greek astronomer Ptolemy. Use the clues to work out which is the correct picture for Gemini.

* The constellation contains at least 15 stars.
* The left hand "twin" has only two stars on each leg.
* The righthand "twin" has one leg longer than the other.
* The "twins" are holding hands.

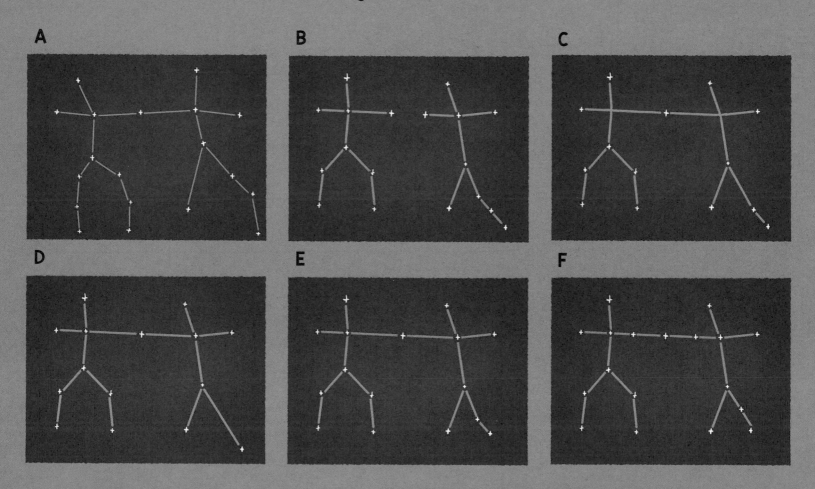

A   B   C

D   E   F

The name Gemini means "twins" in Latin.

The two stars that form the "head" of each twin are called Castor and Pollux. Pollux is the brightest star in the constellation.

44

SOFT LANDING

NASA uses parachutes attached to its reusable equipment to help it fall gently to Earth. Can you find the parachutes described here?

* Three red and white striped parachutes together.
* A single white parachute with a solo star on it.
* A group of three plain turquoise parachutes.

Parachutes can also be used to help exploration rovers land safely on the surface of other planets such as Mars.

FLOATING AROUND

Uh oh! Someone forgot to fasten down the toothbrushes in the ISS! Count how many there are in this jumbled mess.

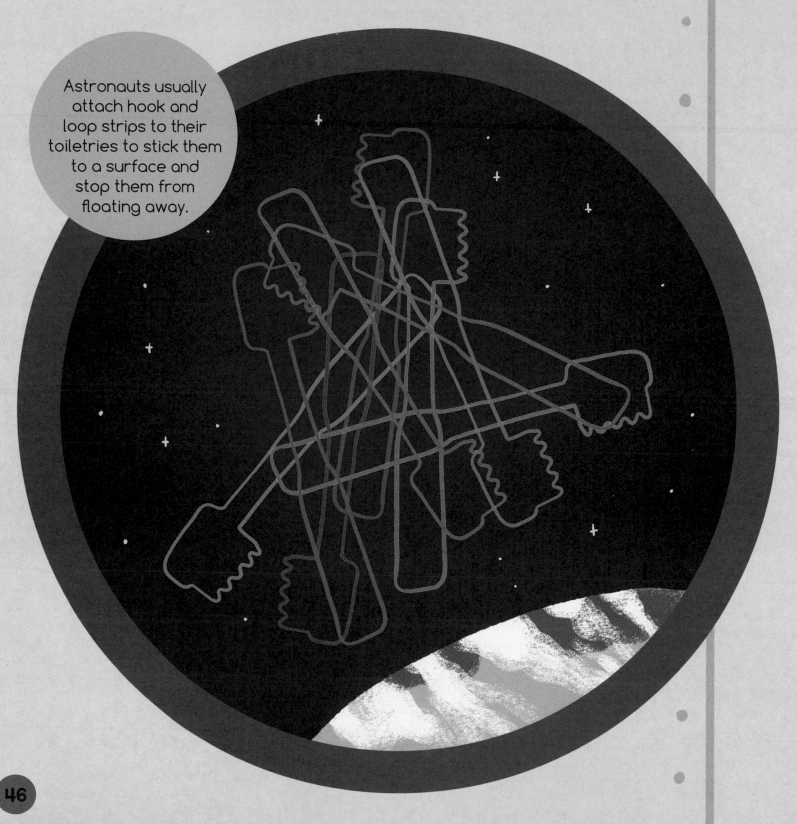

Astronauts usually attach hook and loop strips to their toiletries to stick them to a surface and stop them from floating away.

STUDIES IN SPACE

Astronauts carry out all kinds of experiments and studies while they are on the ISS. Use the clues to work out what each of the astronauts is in charge of, and what country they come from.

Anton

* Shannon and Scott are from the continent of North America.
* The Russian is carrying out Earth studies.
* The Canadian is doing health research.
* Shannon is studying cell growth.
* Sunita is not doing Earth studies.

Sunita

Scott

	USA	Russia	Canada	Germany
Shannon				
Anton				
Sunita				
Scott				

Shannon

	Cell growth	Earth studies	Health research	Microgravity effects
Shannon				
Anton				
Sunita				
Scott				

SPACEWALK

Astronauts sometimes have to leave their spacecraft to perform repairs outside. They usually stay linked by a tether that is fixed to the craft. Work out which of these astronauts isn't tethered to the main ship.

An activity done outside a spacecraft is called a spacewalk or an EVA (extravehicular activity).

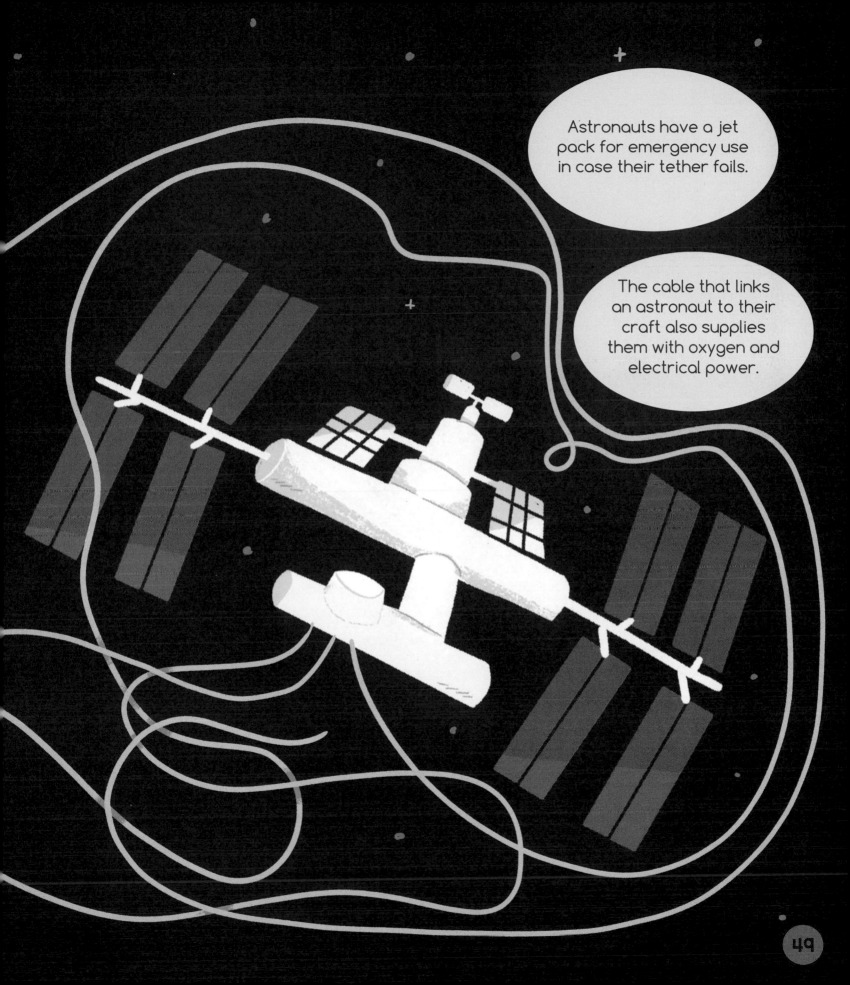

MISSION MEMORIES

Astronauts wear a special patch on their space suit to identify and commemorate which flight they are on. These are from a Russian mission on a Vostok craft. Which of the mission patches is slightly different from the others?

Vostok was a series of early missions to carry Russian astronauts (called cosmonauts) into low Earth orbit. The missions began in the early 1960s.

SATURN'S RINGS

Guide the astronaut safely to Saturn avoiding the ice crystals and storms.

START

Saturn's rings are made up of dust, ice, and rocks.

FINISH

Saturn is the second largest planet in our Solar System. Only Jupiter is bigger. Saturn sits in between Jupiter and Uranus.

Saturn isn't made of rock, like Earth, but gas (mostly hydrogen and helium). It has no surface to land on.

PHOTO OPPORTUNITY

Malik's family are visiting Kennedy Space Center in Florida. The Rocket Garden is amazing! Look at the aerial map and work out which of the photos is the real one that Malik took.

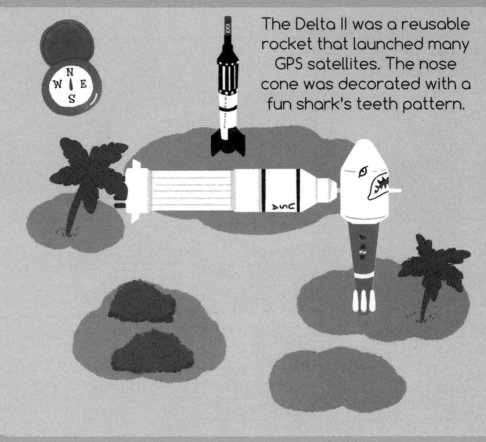

The Delta II was a reusable rocket that launched many GPS satellites. The nose cone was decorated with a fun shark's teeth pattern.

A   B   C   D

IN THE MIDDLE

Early astronomers thought that the Sun revolved around the Earth. In the early 1500s, a Polish astronomer proposed a new theory. His name was Copernicus and he changed our understanding of the Universe. Can you spot eleven differences between these two pictures?

ANIMALS ON HIGH

The clearest stars were arranged into named groups by ancient astronomers. These groups are called constellations and some of them have Latin animal names. Use the clues to match each picture to its Latin name.

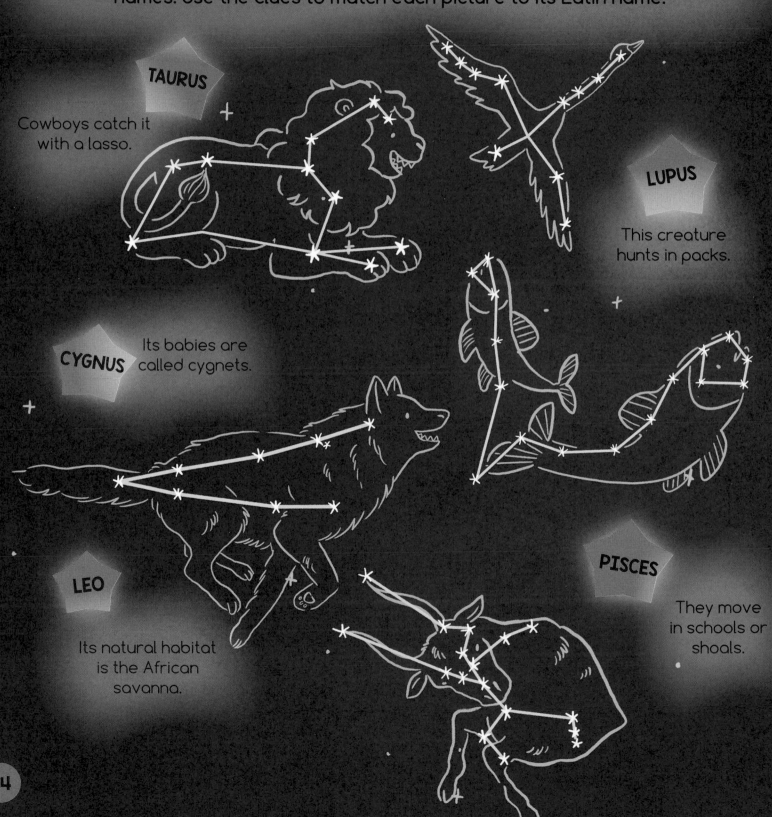

TAURUS

Cowboys catch it with a lasso.

LUPUS

This creature hunts in packs.

CYGNUS Its babies are called cygnets.

LEO

Its natural habitat is the African savanna.

PISCES

They move in schools or shoals.

PRACTICE ON EARTH

Astronauts have to train so they can perform tasks in the strange surroundings of space. This astronaut is in a pool called a neutral buoyancy lab. Can you put the mixed-up picture pieces in the correct order?

1	2	3	4	5	6	7	8	9	10

An astronaut may spend up to seven hours underwater.
The floating motion helps them become used to floating
in space when they perform a spacewalk, or EVA
(extravehicular activity).

FLOATING FRUIT

It's fun for the astronauts to try things in space that are affected by weightlessness. Some have even learned to juggle! Compare these two pictures. Which two fruits have floated away in the second picture?

A

B

Astronauts on the ISS experience weightlessness. It makes them, and all their belongings that aren't fixed in place, float around.

STAR GAZING

You don't have to be a professional astronomer to study the night sky. You can look with your bare eyes, or through binoculars or a telescope. Which one of these silhouettes is an exact match for the main picture?

If you look at the sky at night, you will see lots and lots of stars, but should see some planets, too. Planets shine brighter than most stars, and they don't twinkle.

The darker the sky, the more you will see. The darkness of the sky is measured on the Bortle scale. Class 1 is the darkest and Class 9 is light, seen in built-up areas.

A

B

C

D

E

F

BRAIN POWER

Becoming an astronaut is EXTREMELY competitive. Applicants have to be able to carry out all kinds of different tasks. Here is an example of the type of puzzle that forms part of ESA's selection process. Look at the grid below. Which combination of shapes should fill the gap in the middle?

Astronaut candidates are tested on their logic skills, mental arithmetic, visual perception, and also concentration, teamwork, and leadership.

CRACK THE CODE

Can you enter the correct launch code on the keypad?
Work out the sequence to fill in the blanks on each row, and
then enter the numbers in the spaces below.

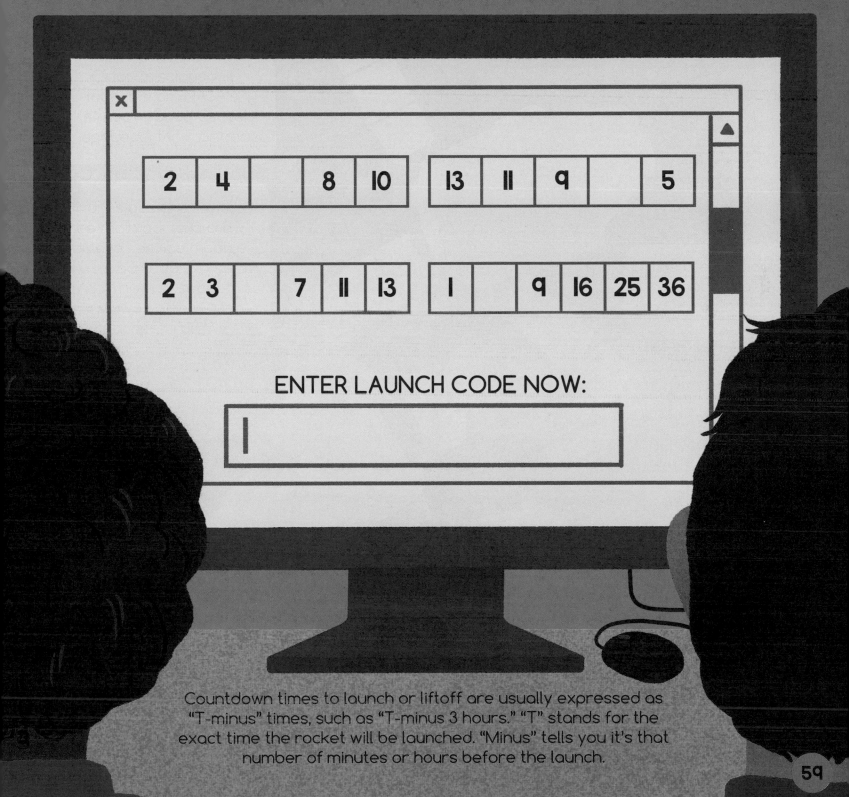

2	4		8	10

13	11	9		5

2	3		7	11	13

1		9	16	25	36

ENTER LAUNCH CODE NOW:

|

Countdown times to launch or liftoff are usually expressed as
"T-minus" times, such as "T-minus 3 hours." "T" stands for the
exact time the rocket will be launched. "Minus" tells you it's that
number of minutes or hours before the launch.

WHICH WAY?

The ISS uses specialist terms to describe directions. Look at the directions in the key, which are listed in opposing pairs. Can you complete the diagram?

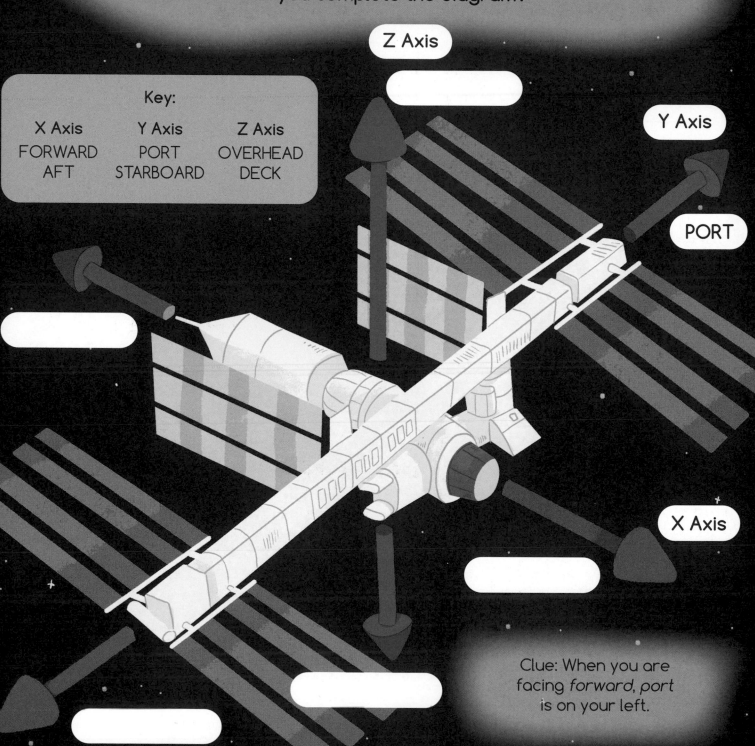

Z Axis

Key:

X Axis	Y Axis	Z Axis
FORWARD	PORT	OVERHEAD
AFT	STARBOARD	DECK

Y Axis

PORT

X Axis

Clue: When you are facing *forward*, *port* is on your left.

IN CONTROL

Part of NASA's training for astronauts involves learning how to pilot a plane. Check out these controls and then turn the page to put your memory to the test.

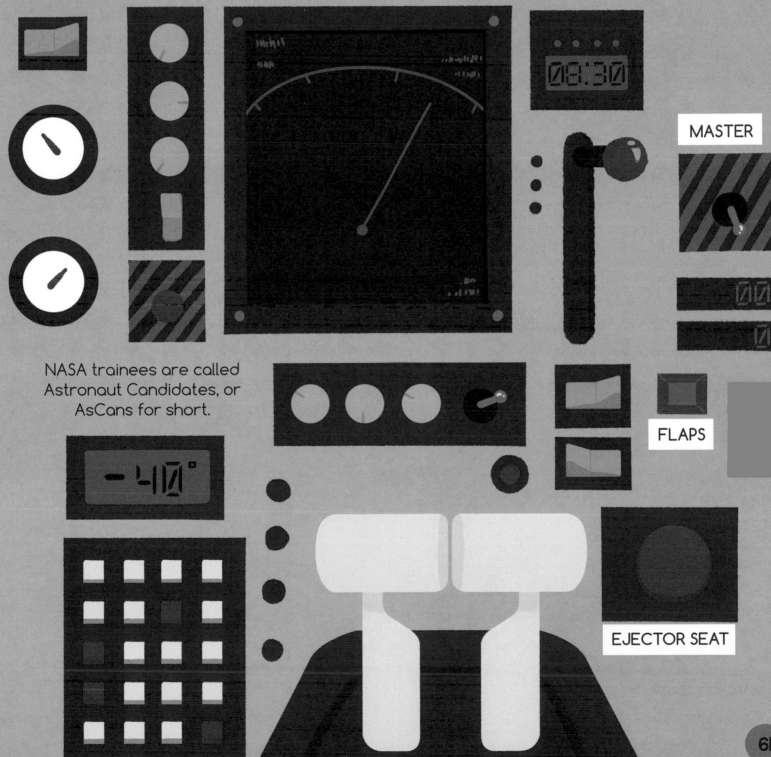

NASA trainees are called Astronaut Candidates, or AsCans for short.

MASTER

FLAPS

EJECTOR SEAT

Can you answer the questions below
without turning back to page 61?

* What time is it?
* What is the current external temperature?
* How many of these dials are there?

* On which side is the ejector seat button—left or right?
* Is the yellow and black MASTER switch flicked up or down?
* Is the button that says FLAPS red or yellow?

Lots of applicants for NASA
have already completed
their pilot training, but it isn't
necessary to have done so
before applying.

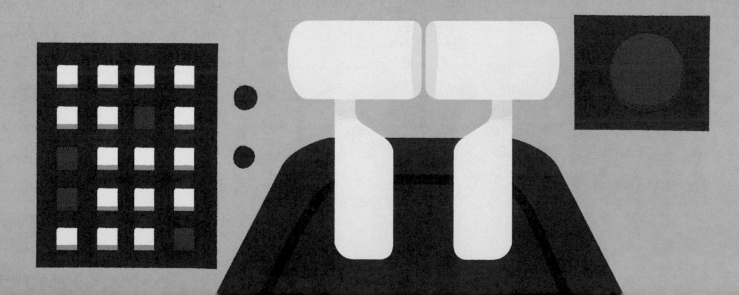

SEARCHING THE SUN

NASA has launched a solar probe called Parker to explore the Sun! It will enter the Sun's corona, and send back images and measurements. Which of these silhouettes exactly matches the main picture?

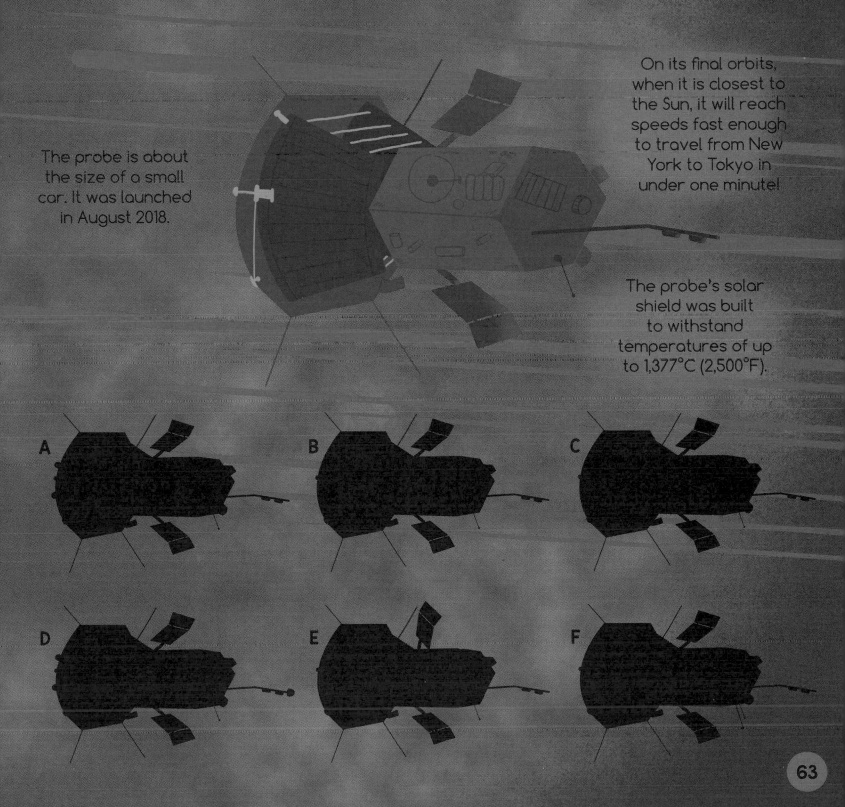

The probe is about the size of a small car. It was launched in August 2018.

On its final orbits, when it is closest to the Sun, it will reach speeds fast enough to travel from New York to Tokyo in under one minute!

The probe's solar shield was built to withstand temperatures of up to 1,377°C (2,500°F).

A

B

C

D

E

F

MAKING CONTACT

Supplies can be sent to the ISS in a small cargo capsule. The capsule has to line up accurately with the docking target. Which one of the docking rings will fit exactly if it is rotated?

The Dragon spacecraft is a reusable robotic vehicle designed by the SpaceX company. It can carry supplies or people to the ISS.

A

B

C

D

JOINT PROJECT

Several nations have joined forces to put the ISS into space. Unscramble the letters to work out the name of some of those countries below.

The principal space agencies involved in the ISS project are those of the United States, Russia, Europe, Japan, and Canada.

WYNORA

SURIAS

PAINS

DAANCA

NEWSED

AJANP

LIATY

LEGIMUB

MADNERK

NCRAFE

NAYGERM

FAR, FAR AWAY

You can see some planets with your own eyes, but it is easier to spot them using a telescope. How many telescopes can you count in this pile?

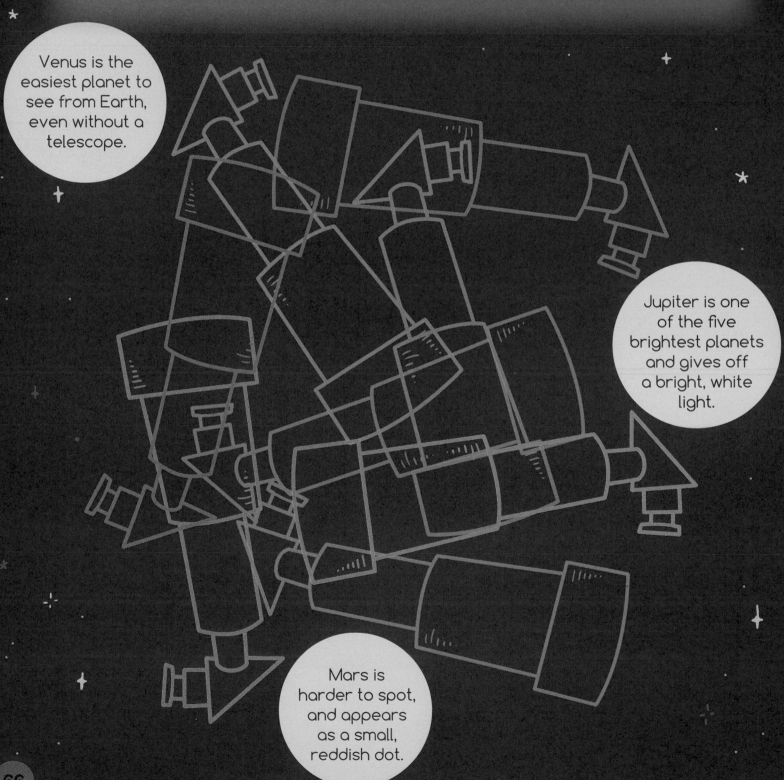

Venus is the easiest planet to see from Earth, even without a telescope.

Jupiter is one of the five brightest planets and gives off a bright, white light.

Mars is harder to spot, and appears as a small, reddish dot.

MANY MOONS

Earth has just one Moon but Jupiter has lots of them. Study these moons carefully and then turn the page.

A moon is a natural object that orbits around a planet.

The first four moons to be discovered (apart from Earth's Moon) were the four Galilean moons of Jupiter. They were named after the Italian astronomer Galileo Galilei.

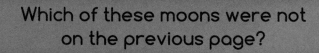

Which of these moons were not
on the previous page?

The Galilean moons are
Io, Europa, Ganymede
and Callisto. They are
Jupiter's largest moons.

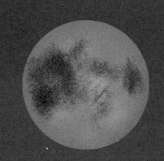

68

FAMOUS NAMES

Caroline and William Herschel were a sister and brother who both became famous astronomers in the eighteenth century. Which is the only group of letters that can be rearranged to spell their surname correctly?

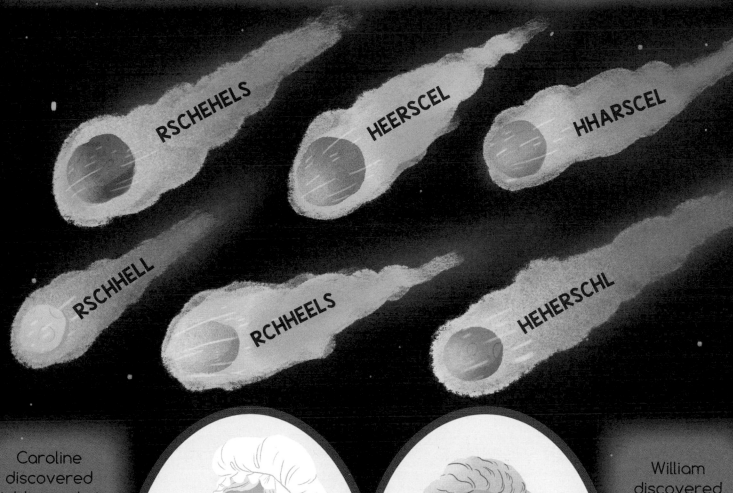

RSCHEHELS

HEERSCEL

HHARSCEL

RSCHHELL

RCHHEELS

HEHERSCHL

Caroline discovered eight comets in total between 1786 and 1797, and also discovered three new nebulae (interstellar clouds made of gas and dust).

William discovered the planet Uranus in 1781. It was the first planet to be discovered for thousands of years.

SIXTEEN SUNRISES

Astronauts on the ISS see the Sun rise 15 or 16 times each day! Which one of these pictures is slightly different from the others?

The ISS completes one trip around the globe every 92 minutes. It travels at 27,700 km (17,200 miles) per hour.

EMERGENCY LANDING

This is the kind of test that astronaut candidates might be given. See how you do!

Your craft has crash-landed on the Moon. Lots of your equipment is damaged or missing, but there are some pieces left. You need to walk to a lunar base at some distance away. Use the clues to decide which five items you should take with you. Which should you leave behind and why?

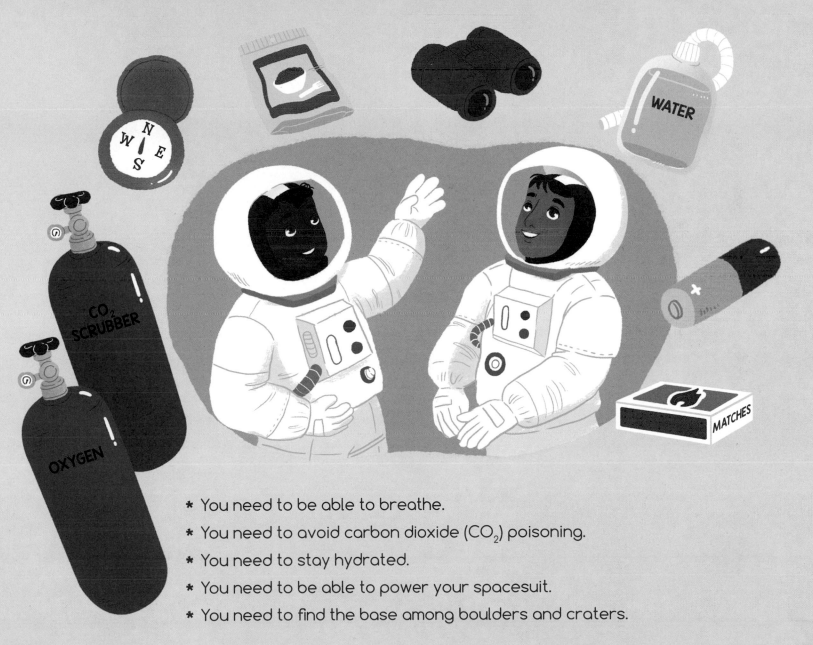

* You need to be able to breathe.
* You need to avoid carbon dioxide (CO_2) poisoning.
* You need to stay hydrated.
* You need to be able to power your spacesuit.
* You need to find the base among boulders and craters.

PLAY TIME

Astronauts work hard, but are allowed some relaxation time each day. Put the missing circles back into this scene. Which one of the circles doesn't fit?

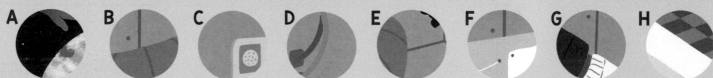

In 2008, chess enthusiast and astronaut Greg Chamitoff played a game of chess against a team of students on Earth— 337 km (210 mi) below him.

The pieces have Velcro to fix them to the board. Magnetic pieces would interfere with other high-tech equipment on the spacecraft.

SPATIAL AWARENESS

Trainee astronauts get tested for their ability to form a mental picture of an object and move it around with their imagination. It can help with living and working in the weightlessness of space, where there is no up or down. Test yourself with these questions.

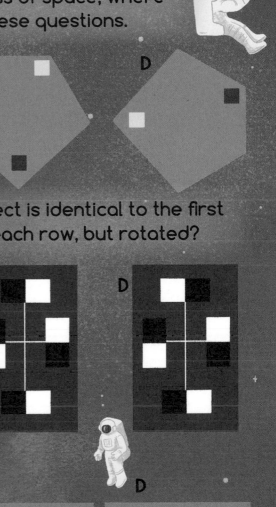

A   B   C   D

Which object is identical to the first one in each row, but rotated?

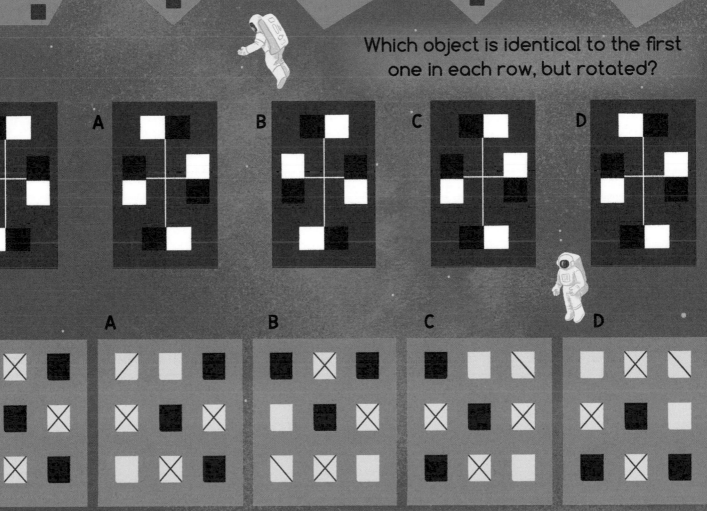

A   B   C   D

A   B   C   D

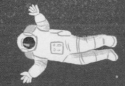

This kind of mental manipulation is also a great skill for technical jobs, or jobs where you will need to follow directions or imagine items in three dimensions.

SPACE SORTER

Match the facts to the little pictures, and find a way to fill the grid so that each row, column, and mini-grid contains one of each picture.

All four giant **planets** in our Solar System have rings.

Stars in a **constellation** look close together but are really huge distances apart.

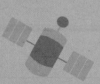

A whole bunch of **shooting stars** together is called a meteor shower.

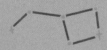

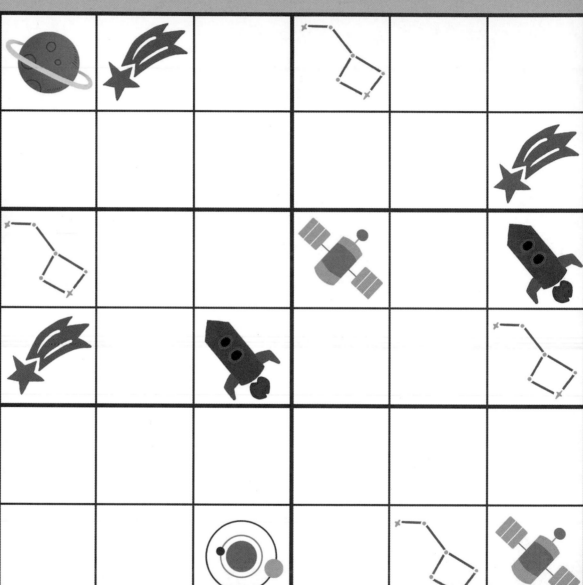

Rocket engines need an explosive chemical reaction to push them through Earth's atmosphere.

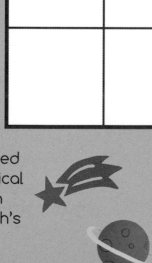

The **Solar System** is around 4.5 billion years old.

The main part of a **satellite** is called a bus. Other parts are attached to it.

ESCAPE HATCH

Help the astronaut float her way from her current location
to the open hatch.

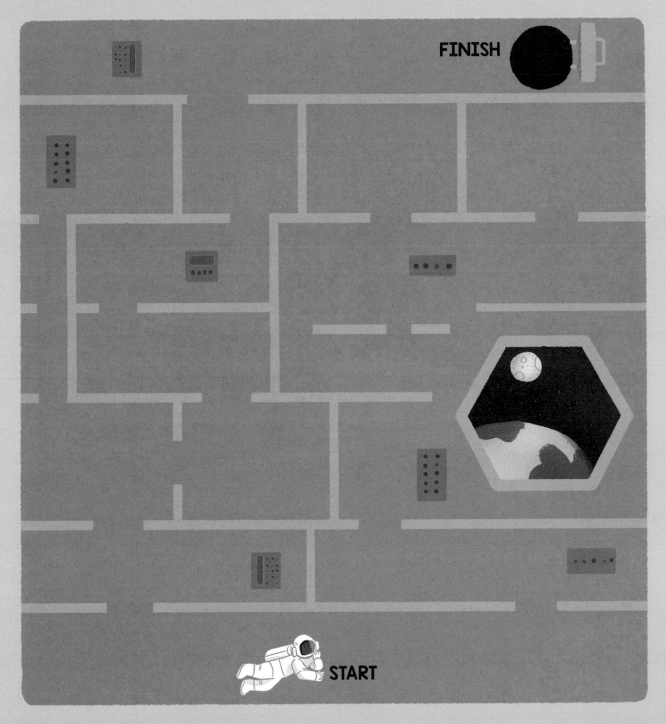

External doors use an airlock to allow astronauts to move between places that have
different pressure. When leaving the ISS for an EVA, for example, the astronaut has
to seal airtight doors on each side of a compartment before exiting the craft.

ASTRONAUT TEST

Here's another visual and spatial awareness test for you to
see if you have what it takes to become an astronaut one day!

Which of the groups of shapes can be assembled to make the large shape shown above them?

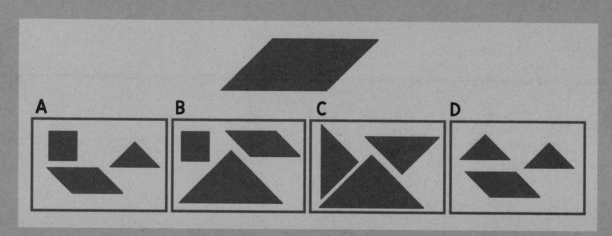

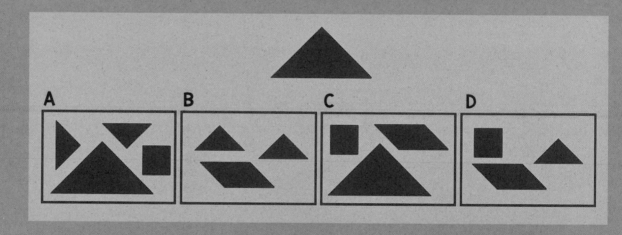

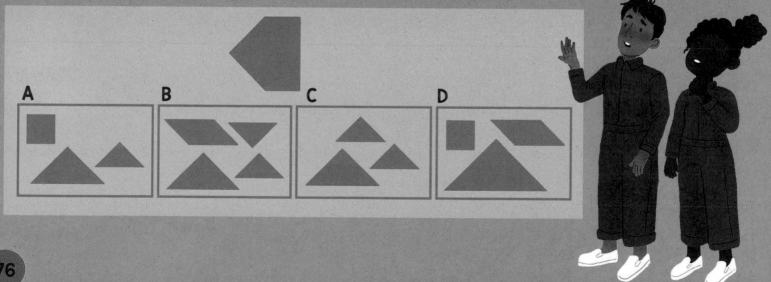

LIFE ON OTHER PLANETS

Could there be other planets with living things on them? We don't know what these living things might look like; they could be so small they can only be seen with a microscope. Study this page and then turn over to test your memory.

Astronomers are constantly looking for other planets like ours, but outside our Solar System. They call them exoplanets.

The "habitable zone" is the area around a star where the temperature is right to potentially have liquid water on the planet's surface.

Scientists study space for planets about the same size as Earth within their star's "habitable zone" as these are the best places to look for living things.

How many of this creature did you count on the previous page?

Which two creatures on this page are new?

How has this creature changed?

Was this one there?

Which creature is missing?

LIVING ON MARS

Could future space research allow us to live on Mars? There are many challenges involved, but it is some people's dream. Can you find all these items hidden in this artist's idea of life on the Red Planet?

One of the goals of the SpaceX company is to help humans get to Mars.

SPACE TRAINING

Astronaut training involves many different things, long before you enter an actual spacecraft. Work your way around the space training course following the instructions.

The precision air-bearing floor helps astronauts learn how to move large objects in space, where there is no friction to make them stop. It is like a huge air hockey table.

Trainees spend hours underwater in the neutral buoyancy laboratory, moving in a similar way to moving in space.

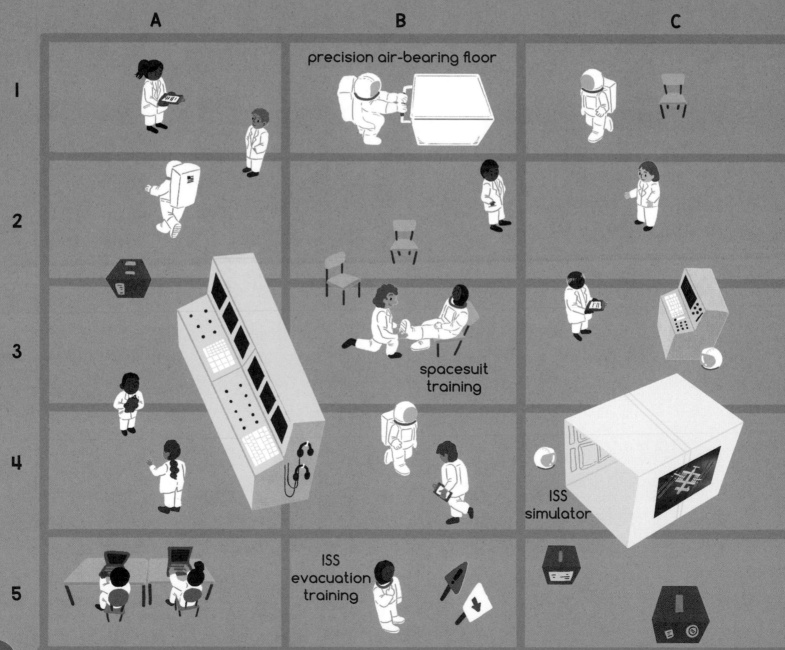

precision air-bearing floor

spacesuit training

ISS simulator

ISS evacuation training

I square = 10-minute walk

TRAINING SCHEDULE:

1. Start in A2. Head to the centrifuge. How many squares have you been in? Which training session did you pass?

2. Walk two squares to reach the ground-based spacewalk. What grid reference is that?

3. Now you need to get to the ISS Simulator. How long will that take?

4. Walk to C5. Your next session is 20 minutes to the right. Where are you heading?

5. Your final training sessions are in E3 then B3. If the first finishes at 16:00 and you need 20 minutes to get dried and changed, what time will you arrive at the last session if you take the quickest route?

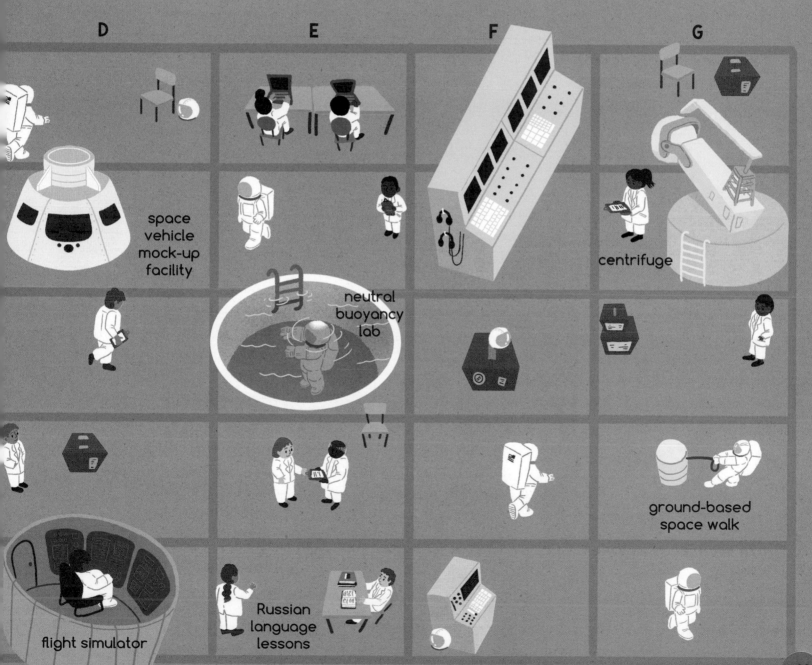

SPACE SELFIE!

An astronaut's helmet has an extremely reflective surface. You can see this one's gloves and camera as she takes a selfie! Take a look at the two photographs and see if you can spot eight differences.

CRAZY CRATERS

In 2013 the Chinese Space Agency landed their first rover on the Moon. It covered a total distance of 114 m (374 ft) investigating the Moon's surface, and stayed operational for 31 months. Find a path through the craters to 31 following a prime number sequence.

The lunar rover was called *Yutu* and was part of the Chang'e 3 mission to the Moon. The spacecraft was named after the goddess of the Moon in Chinese mythology, and the rover after her pet rabbit.

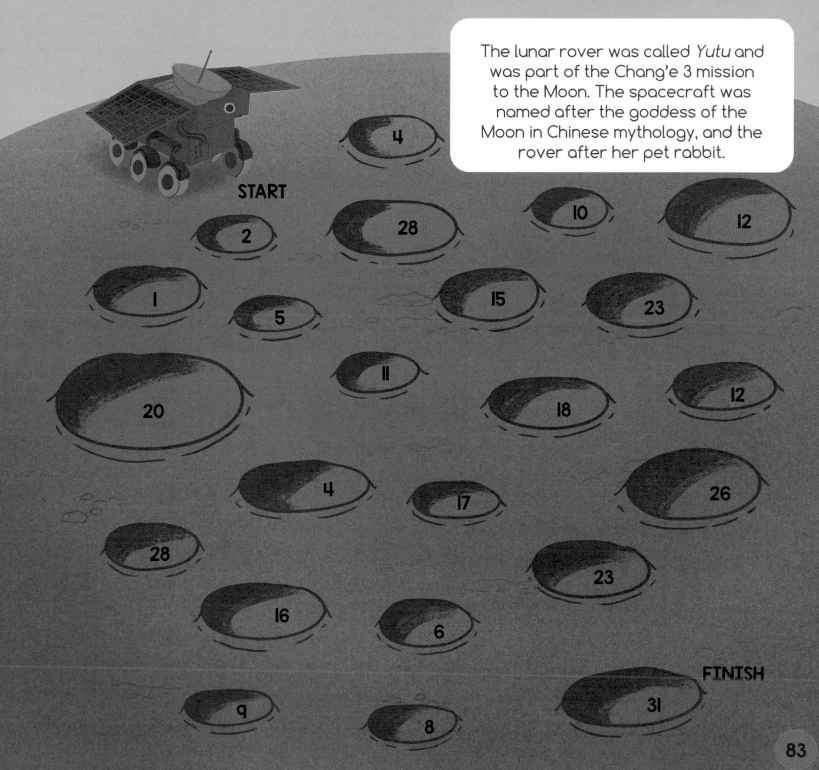

START

FINISH

THE SPACE RACE

Space exploration started with fierce rivalry between nations, but space missions are much friendlier these days. Follow the correct chronological path from start to finish and you'll be taken on a journey of amazing space firsts and feats.

1957
First satellite launched: Sputnik (Soviet Union).

START

Nov 1965
First French rocket launched.

July 1965
First Mars flyby (USA).

1959
First probe to reach the Moon (Soviet Union).

1963
First woman in space (Soviet Union).

1961
First person to fly in space (Soviet Union).

Dec 1962
First interplanetary flyby (USA).

Sept 1962
First Canadian satellite launched.

HAPPY BIRTHDAY!

What do you do when you have your birthday in space? Celebrate! One ISS astronaut had macarons delivered for his birthday. How many of the treats can you find in this picture?

The astronaut in question was Thomas Pesquet from France. NASA sent the French delicacies—along with Thomas' beloved saxophone—in a cargo craft.

HAPPY BIRTHDAY!

ANSWERS

Page 4

Page 5

Mike has spent the longest on board, and Sandra the least time.
This is the correct order:
Mike, Peggy, Yuri, Sunita, Koichi, Sandra.

Page 6

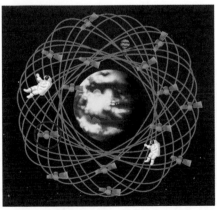

Page 7

The correct order is: 2, 9, 1, 8, 6, 4, 3, 10, 7, 5.

Page 8

Page 10

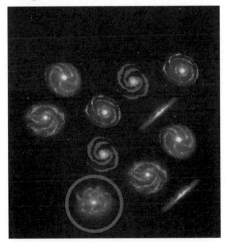

Page 11

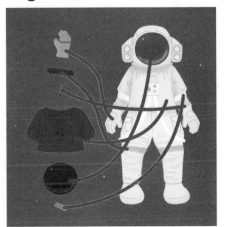

Page 12

A hammer and a screwdriver are missing.

Page 13

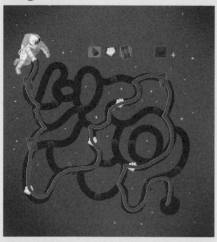

Page 14

Page 15

Page 16

Box B contains all of the parts to make the robotic arm.

Page 17

The dwarf planets are:
ERIS
PLUTO

Pages 18-19

Squares A, E, G, I, and J are not on the main picture.

Page 20

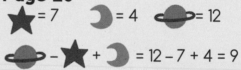

★ = 7   ☽ = 4   🪐 = 12

🪐 − ★ + ☽ = 12 − 7 + 4 = 9

Page 21

Page 22

This is the correct order from biggest to smallest:
FAST in China
Effelsberg in Germany
Lovell in England
DSS in Australia
The Sardinian telescope (in Italy)

Page 23

The red and black wire connects A to F.
The wire from terminal D is loose.
One wire from B is connected to an orange terminal (H).
The red battery needs to be changed to make the green light work.
There are four striped wires.

Pages 24-25

Page 26

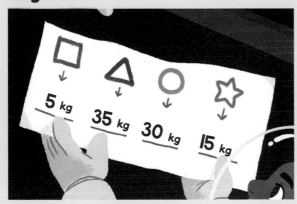

Page 27

Page 28

Page 29

There should be 2 candidates circled.

Page 30

Wheel B will turn clockwise.

Page 31

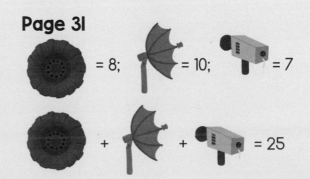

= 8; = 10; = 7

+ + = 25

Pages 32-33

Page 34

	Belka	Strelka	Laika	Dezik	Tsygan
1951				✔	✔
1957			✔		
1960	✔	✔			

Page 35

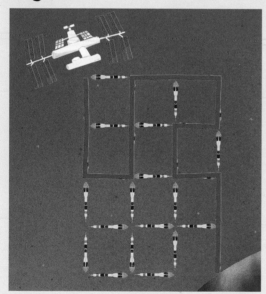

Page 36

Pages 37-38

These stars were added:

This star disappeared:

Page 39

TRIPEJU

Page 40
D is a little bit different.

Page 41
Box C contains all the correct parts.

Page 42

Page 43
D is the matching silhouette.

Page 44
D is the correct picture for Gemini.

Page 45
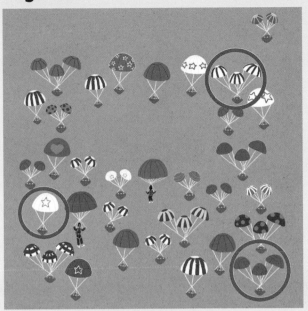

Page 46
There are 9 toothbrushes.

Page 47
Shannon—USA—cell growth
Anton—Russia—Earth studies
Sunita—Germany—microgravity effects
Scott—Canada—health research

Pages 48–49

Page 50
Mission patch B is slightly different from the others.

Page 51

Page 52
Malik took photograph C.

Page 53

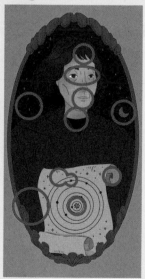

Page 54
Leo—lion
Taurus—bull
Cygnus—swan
Lupus—wolf
Pisces—fish

Page 55

The correct order is 2, 7, 4, 8, 3, 6, 9, 1, 5, 10.

Page 56

Page 57
Picture E is an exact match.

Page 58
C is the correct combination.

Page 59
2, 4, 6, 8, 10 (increasing even numbers)
13, 11, 9, 7, 5 (decreasing odd numbers)

2, 3, 5, 7, 11, 13 (the first prime numbers)
1, 4, 9, 16, 25, 36 (square numbers, e.g. 2 x 2)

ENTER LAUNCH CODE NOW: 6 7 5 4

Page 60

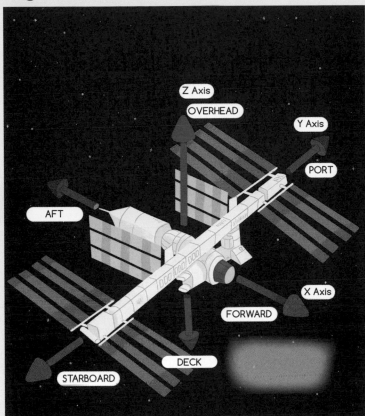

Page 61
The time is 8.30.
The current external temperature is –40°C.
There are two dials.
The ejector seat button is on the right.
The yellow and black MASTER switch is flicked down.
The button that says FLAPS is red.

Page 63
Silhouette C is an exact match.

Page 64
Docking ring D will fit exactly.

Page 65
NORWAY
SPAIN
SWEDEN
BELGIUM
DENMARK
FRANCE
GERMANY
ITALY
JAPAN
CANADA
RUSSIA

Page 66
There are 8 telescopes in the pile.

Page 67

Page 69
RCHHEELS

Page 70
Picture G is slightly different.

Page 71

These are the items you should take:

Oxygen CO_2 scrubber Water Battery Binoculars

You should definitely take the oxygen canister and the water because you won't get far without those.

You'll also need the carbon-dioxide scrubber canister to remove the carbon dioxide you breathe out—otherwise, you will die of carbon-dioxide poisoning.

Take the battery as your spacesuit needs power for the ventilation and cooling systems.

Take the binoculars so that you can scan the horizon for the base and plan your route to it.

You won't need these items:

Compass Matches Dehydrated food

Leave behind the compass as that only works on Earth.

Definitely leave behind the matches as there is no oxygen for them to burn.

You can't eat while wearing a spacesuit, so don't bother with the dehydrated food.

Page 72

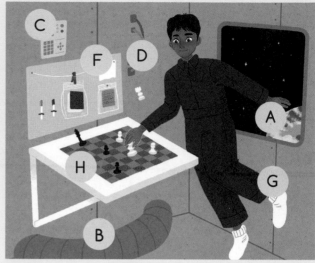

Circle E doesn't fit.

Page 73

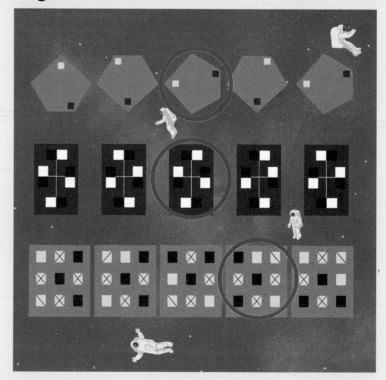

94

Page 74

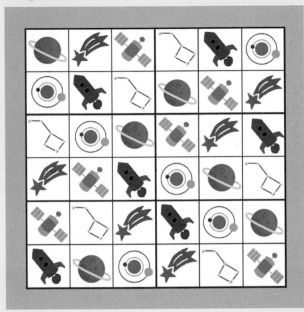

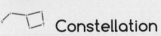 Planet

Rocket

Constellation

Solar system

Shooting star

Satellite

Page 75

Page 76
C
B
B

Page 78

 There are two of this creature on the previous page.

  These two creatures are new on this page.

 Yes, this one is on the previous page.

This creature now has an antenna.

This creature is missing.

Page 79

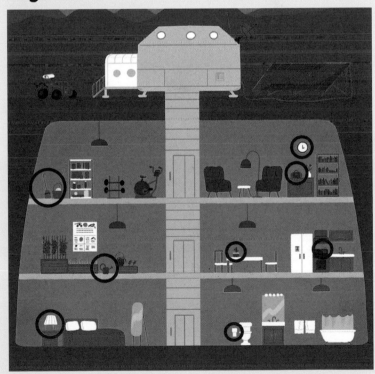

Pages 80–81

1. 7 squares; the space vehicle mock-up facility
2. G4
3. 40 minutes
4. To E5—Russian language lessons.
5. 16:50

Page 82

Page 83

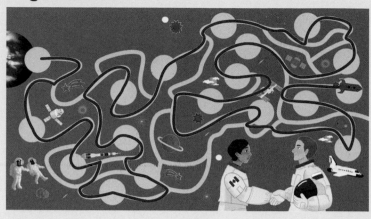

The path follows alternate prime numbers.

Page 86

There are 11 treats.